Unstoppable Me: Living With Epilepsy

Copyright © 2021 by Beauty From Ashes, LLC

ISBN: 978-0-578-93554-6

Illustrated By: I.G.R.P.Karunarathna

All rights reserved.

No part of this book may be reproduced or transmitted in any form or by any means without written permission.

Photo credits: NV Models & Talent

Dedication and Acknowledgements

This is dedicated to my Paw Paw (Boyde Marr) and Ganny (Delores Farley) who if they are watching over me, I know they are smiling right now. I know they would be supportive and proud of me. I love you forever and ever and ever until the next page!

God: Thank you for allowing me to have a beautiful life. I will never forget the day you changed my life!

My parents, Jermaine and Carrie Farley: Thank you for trying your hardest to make every event, play, and moment of my life. Mommy thank you for exposing me to so many different things in life.

My brother and sister: Ja'vonte aka Tay Tay and Calynn…thank you for supporting me and for trying to come to all of my events.

Nana: Thank you for supporting and taking care of me. You are always there!

NV Models & Talent: Thanks especially to Ron and Chester for believing in me and taking a chance on me when Ms. Wones recommended ….Ms. Wones…THANK YOU!

Epilepsy Kids Crew: Thank you for changing my life and showing me that having epilepsy isn't so bad and exposing me to other kids who have it and are cool!

Bishop and Mother Lash: Thank you for your prayers and for coming to see me at my plays. I love you!

Special Cousins: Denise, Debi, Taylor, David, and Mar-Mar…thank you for coming to my events, supporting me and praying for me during my seizures, and giving me a get-away when life got crazy.

Teachers: Ms. Myers, Ms. Frye, Ms. Wright (Madison Park), Ms. Blakenship and Ms. Moore (Westbrooke Drama Club)), and Mrs. Troutman, Ms. Latham, and Ms. Brunk (ELC)

Coach Marie Marcellus: Thank you for coaching me on the field and teaching me lit cheers.

Director: Mr. Jason Hampton, Ms. Philitia Charlton, Mr. Thomas Troutman….THANK YOU for believing in my talent and picking me to play the roles you assigned me. I love you forever!

Special Mention: My Gahmie, Latoria Henderson for supporting me. Tyrin Turner, Charnae the Voice, and Loretta Troutman…thank you for your words of wisdom on set and for encouraging me.

Special Friends: EJ, Imani and Naomi Jones…thank you guys for supporting me and coming to watch my performances

Ms. Taja Simpson and Mr. AJ Joiner: Thank you for always encouraging me to manifest my goals, and that I can talk to you whenever and you always write me back and never ignore me. May God bless you both, and "see you on set!"

Living With Epilepsy One night while I was sleeping, I had a **seizure**. I was so scared while my mother took me to the hospital. I had to get a needle in my arm, also known as an **IV**. I was able to go home, get some rest and sleep peacefully.

Three weeks later, the same thing happened again—except this time was a little worse than the other. I was back in the hospital with another **IV** in my arm, and some tests being done on my head called an **EEG**. I had to wear it for 24 hours. I could not even stay at school for that day, but I smiled through it all! I was given my **diagnosis** of **Rolandic Benign Epilepsy with Centrotemporal Spikes or BECTS**.

In 2018 on Christmas Eve, the worst happened: I had another **seizure** that was worse than the other ones. My mouth was twisted, and my right side was very weak and I could not move. It was the worst day of my life! The doctors wanted me to stay another night so they could watch me, but I was so sad and nervous to miss Christmas Day with my family, so they let me go home with another 24 hour **EEG monitor**.

With the new **medicine** that I had to take to control the number of **seizures** I was having, I started having **side effects** on top of the after-effects from my **seizures**. I started getting bad grades in writing because my hands would shake when I tried to write anything. I became **confused** about completing my assignments, tests, and even with what I was being asked to do at home by my parents and Nana. I was put on a **504 plan** by my parents and the team at school so that I can continue to be protected with the support I need to continue doing good in school.

After my **neurologist** referred me, I was able to get **occupational therapy** to learn how to write better and **concentrate** a little more.

Even with all of my **confusion**, and hard times trying to put my clothes and shoes on the right way, I did not let that stop me! Living with **epilepsy**, I have been able to be a cheerleader for three years (before COVID-19). I also participated in a dance recital where I had a lead in one of our dances.

I have been able to act—where I had **auditioned** and earned multiple roles in two plays: "The Wiz" and "Death of a Lie." I also auditioned for and landed a mini role in a scene in the movie <u>Love, Loyalty & Death</u>. I am BLESSED how God allows me to remember my lines every time that I **perform**!

Last but definitely not least, I have been a model with NV Models & Talent for four years now, and have been able to model for online ads such as Swim Outlet.

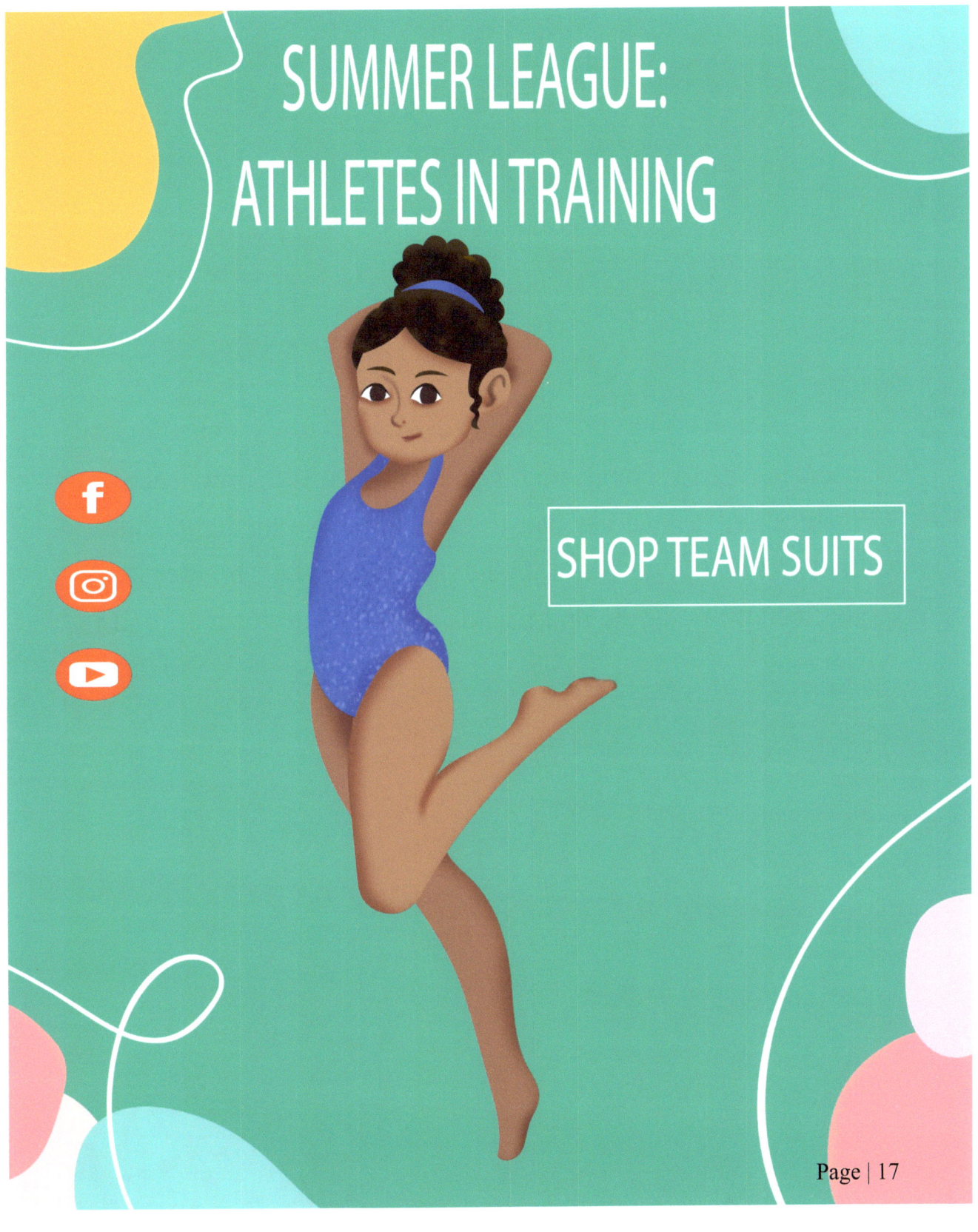

I started having fewer **seizures**, so my **neurologist** decided that I could finally be taken off of my seizure medication! I have not had to take any more medicine since January 2020! My Nana, Father, Mother, sister, brother, and the rest of my family and friends are so happy for me…and I am too!

To any kids out there—even adults who have **epilepsy**, another kind of **disability** or struggle, whatever you do, do NOT let it stop you from doing whatever you want to do or what you were created to be…we got this!

Glossary

Epilepsy- a neurological disorder marked by sudden recurrent episodes of sensory disturbance, loss of consciousness, or convulsions, associated with abnormal electrical activity in the brain.

Seizure- a sudden, uncontrolled electrical disturbance in the brain. It can cause changes in your behavior, movements or feelings, and in levels of consciousness.

IV- an apparatus used to administer a fluid (as of medication, blood, or nutrients) intravenously; also: a fluid administered by IV.

EEG- a test that detects abnormalities in your brain waves, or in the electrical activity of your brain.

Diagnosis- the art or act of identifying a disease from its signs and symptoms.

Benign Rolandic Epilepsy with Centrotemporal Spikes, or BECTS-seizures that involve twitching, numbness, or tingling of the face or tongue. Also focal seizures—meaning they only occur on one side of the brain at a time.

Medicine- a substance or preparation used in treating disease.

Side effects- a secondary, typically undesirable effect of a drug or medical treatment.

Confusion- difficulty in understanding or in being able to tell one thing from a similar thing; a feeling or state of uncertainty.

Concentrate- to make something stronger, denser, or more focused.

504 Plan- a **plan** developed to ensure that a child who has a disability identified under the law and is attending an elementary or secondary educational institution receives accommodations that will ensure their academic success and access to the learning environment.

Neurologist- a medical doctor who specializes in treating diseases of the nervous system.

Occupational therapy- a form of therapy for those recuperating from physical or mental illness that encourages rehabilitation through the performance of activities required in daily life.

Auditioned- to test or try out in a short performance.

Performed- discharge, execute, transact mean to carry to completion a prescribed course of action.

Disability- a person who has a physical or mental impairment that substantially limits one or more major life activity.

References

Merriam-Webster's Dictionary
Oxford Languages
Americans with Disabilities Act

Thank you...!

www.ingramcontent.com/pod-product-compliance
Lightning Source LLC
LaVergne TN
LVHW072102070426
835508LV00002B/240